I Will Remember You
Workbook

I Will Remember You

A workbook for anyone ages 8 - 14

who has experienced the death of someone special

Andrea D. Sims

Illustrated by:
Courtney Strickland
and
Lacey Jarrell

Order this book online at www.trafford.com
or email orders@trafford.com

Most Trafford titles are also available at major online book retailers.

Print information available on the last page.

ISBN: 978-1-4120-3969-7 (sc)

Trafford rev. 10/16/2018

www.trafford.com

North America & international
toll-free: 1 888 232 4444 (USA & Canada)
fax: 812 355 4082

Dedication

Dedicated to everyone who has experienced the loss of a loved one and is afraid of forgetting.

Acknowledgments

This book and my day-to-day work would not be possible without the love and support of my husband, Randall. He has gone to bed many nights while I worked on "just one more thing" related to this workbook. Many thanks to Kay Watson who edited, gave helpful suggestions, and encouragement to make this book a reality. I would like to thank my daughter, Laura, who did one final edit, and to Jeremy McBryar, who is my own personal technical support when I have computer problems. I am grateful to my nieces, Courtney Strickland and Lacey Jarrell, who spent hours drawing the illustrations for this book. I also want to thank all the people who have taught me about loss as we took the journey together.

Dear Friend,

I know this is a difficult time for you. I also know that you are experiencing many different feelings as you go through the loss of someone you love. The feelings you are having are normal, even though they may be confusing.

Because it is sometimes easier to write about your feelings than it is to talk about them, I have written some sentence stems that you can finish with your own thoughts and feelings. I hope you will make this book your own by writing things that will help you remember the person who was special to you. You may want to color the pictures, or draw others to help you through this difficult time. You may even want to use the blank pages in the back to write a poem or some other thoughts you have.

You don't have to finish the book now. You may want to put it away for a while then get it out later and work on it, or you may want to write in it as you experience the different feelings listed in bold print at the top of each section.

It is important that you know you can survive this experience. There may be times when you don't think you can, but you CAN. Some common things you may experience are:

- **Continuing to ask WHY**
- **Feeling numb**
- **Not being able to concentrate or remember things**
- **Feeling that this is not real, and that it never happened**
- **Thinking you are going crazy because of what you are thinking or feeling**
- **Your mind won't shut off**
- **Wanting to run somewhere**

- **Feeling guilty when you catch yourself laughing or smiling**
- **Having some good days and then having bad days again**
- **Feeling like you are caught in a storm**

Some people may not understand what you are going through or how you are feeling. It may not be easy for you to talk about your loss, but it is important to find someone who is a good listener. You may feel comfortable talking to a parent, a favorite aunt or uncle, or a neighbor. Your school counselor, if you have one, may be a good person to get to know during this time. It is also very helpful to talk to others who have had a similar experience, and your counselor may have a small group for students who are going through a loss. Talking to someone in a place of worship may also be helpful. I hope you will find someone you feel comfortable taking to about your confusing feelings.

It is important to remember that you do not have to try to be brave. Crying is not a sign of weakness and is a normal way to express grief. It is also important to take care of yourself physically during this time by eating properly and getting enough exercise.

In the back of this workbook, I also listed some titles of books you might want to read. I hope this workbook will be helpful to you during this difficult time.

Sincerely,

Andrea Sims

The Grief Process

- The survivor goes through stages after a loss
- It is possible to be in more than one stage at a time
- Each person moves through the stages in his/her own way and time
- Returning to an earlier stage temporarily is normal

Stages of Loss

Denial/Shock
Feeling numb, not believing the person really died, trouble sleeping, not getting hungry, or trouble concentrating are experienced in this stage.

Emotional Release
In this stage, the survivor is able to cry about the loss.

Depression
In this stage, comes the realization that the person is really gone. Thinking that things are never going to be better is also present in this stage. The survivor may have trouble paying attention, may cry often, and may not be interested in things that usually are interesting. In this stage, there may be a change in eating or sleeping habits, and stomach or headaches may be experienced.

Panic/Fear
In this stage, the survivor may not be able to do the things that need to be done, and may have nightmares or get scared easily.

Guilt/Bargaining

Anyone can think of something to feel guilty about in this stage. The person may say things like, "If only they were here, I would…"

Anger/Resentment

The survivor may be mad at God, the world, friends who are happy, or the person who died, or may be more irritable with others.

Unable to return to a routine

Everything seems too hard, and the survivor wonders if it is worth it to go on.

Acceptance

In this stage, the survivor realizes the person is really gone and knows he/she must continue life without the lost loved one.

Reorganization

The survivor may be a stronger person because of the experience of losing the person. Close relationships with others can be developed without constant fear of getting close to someone. The survivor does not think about the person who died as often and is able to laugh and enjoy things again.

I Will Remember You...

My Name Is: _____ .

My Age Is: _____ .

Today's Date Is: _____ .

This book is written about you and the things I remember.

Your name is _____ .

This is when you were born _____ .

This is when you died _____ .

This is how long it has been since you died _____ .

"When someone dies, you don't get over it by forgetting; you get over it by remembering, and you are aware that no person is ever truly lost or gone once they have been in our life and loved us, as we have loved them."

Leslie Marmon Silko

This is how you died and who was with you...

_____

_____

_____

_____

_____

_____

_____

_____

_____

_____

This story is about who you were and what you meant to me...

_____

_____

_____

_____

_____

_____

_____

_____

_____

_____

_____

Here is something I have written about your life...

_____

_____

_____

_____

_____

_____

_____

_____

_____

_____

Memories Of You

Here are some of the things we did together…

_____

_____

_____

_____

_____

_____

_____

_____

_____

_____

Our best time together was...

_____

_____

_____

_____

_____

_____

_____

_____

_____

_____

_____

Some things you said or did that I will never forget…

_____

_____

_____

_____

_____

_____

_____

_____

_____

_____

_____

The last time we talked or saw one another …

_____

_____

_____

_____

_____

_____

_____

_____

_____

_____

_____

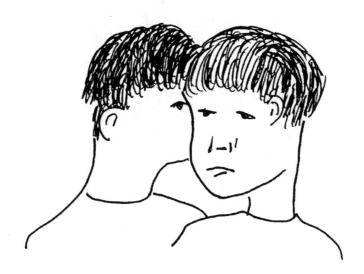

I remember you when I see, smell, or hear...

_____

_____

_____

_____

_____

_____

_____

_____

_____

_____

Here are some songs or words of a song that help me when I am missing you...

_____

_____

_____

_____

_____

_____

_____

_____

_____

_____

Here are some pictures that remind me of you…

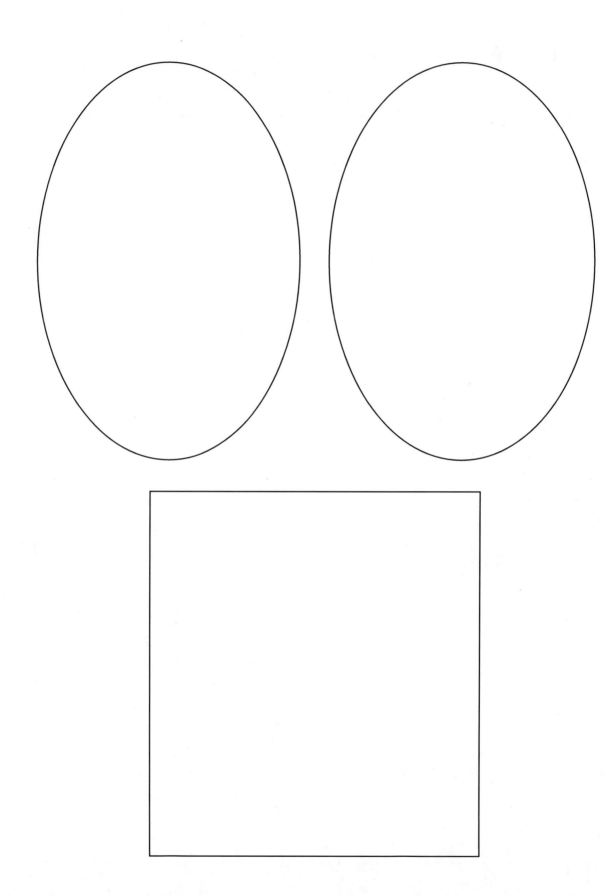

I kept some of your personal things. This is what I have and what they mean to me…

_____

_____

_____

_____

_____

_____

_____

_____

_____

_____

_____

Support

This is someone I can or will talk to about you and your death...

After you died, I wish people had not done or said this...

_____

_____

_____

_____

_____

_____

_____

_____

_____

_____

_____

Here is what I wish people had done to support me...

_____

_____

_____

_____

_____

_____

_____

_____

_____

_____

Some people tried to support me, but I wanted to be left alone because...

_____

_____

_____

_____

_____

_____

_____

_____

_____

_____

_____

Some of my family members and friends who have been there for me during this time are...

_____

_____

_____

_____

_____

_____

_____

_____

_____

_____

One person who helped me a lot after your death was…

_____

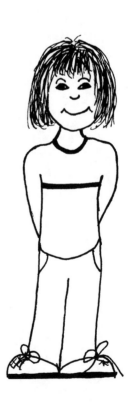

People that I can talk to about how I feel are my…

_____Parents

_____Teachers

_____School counselor

_____Friend

_____Brother

_____Sister

_____Doctor

_____Grandparent

_____Aunt

_____Uncle

_____Neighbor

_____Coach

_____Cousin

_____Spiritual or religious leader

I have people to turn to…

_____For support
_____For friendship
_____For good advice
_____To help me learn
_____To help me do new things
_____To talk to about how I feel
_____To share problems
_____To build me up
_____To accept me
_____For fun

Today I needed comfort
Today I needed strong arms
Today I needed to know someone cared
Today I needed you
Only you were not there

Andrea Sims

Shock And Denial

This is how I felt right after I found out about your death...

_____

_____

_____

_____

_____

_____

_____

_____

_____

_____

Your Service 0r Memorial

This is what your funeral or memorial service was like and how I felt about going...

_____

_____

_____

_____

_____

_____

_____

_____

_____

_____

Here are some things to help me remember your death and funeral service or memorial...

_____

_____

_____

_____

_____

_____

_____

_____

_____

_____

Panic

This is what I worry about or am afraid of...

_____

_____

_____

_____

_____

_____

_____

_____

_____

_____

_____

Release

I was able to cry when...

_____

_____

_____

_____

_____

_____

_____

_____

_____

_____

I seem to cry the most when…

_____

_____

_____

_____

_____

_____

_____

_____

_____

_____

"If tears could build a stairway,
And memories a lane,
I'd walk right up to heaven
And bring you home again."

Unknown

Loneliness

I miss you the most when...

_____

_____

_____

_____

_____

_____

_____

_____

_____

_____

I missed you today
I missed you yesterday and before.
I wanted you today
I wanted to be with you, like before.
I longed for you today
I longed to hear your voice, like before.
I loved you today
I loved you yesterday, and before.

Andrea Sims

Sometimes I want to be left alone because...

_____

_____

_____

_____

_____

_____

_____

_____

_____

_____

Sometimes when I am alone I...

_____

_____

_____

_____

_____

_____

_____

_____

_____

_____

People who care about me are my...

_____ Mother
_____ Father
_____ Grandmother
_____ Grandfather
_____ Cousin
_____ Friend (s)
_____ Teacher
_____ Counselor
_____ Brother
_____ Sister
_____ Coach
_____ Teammates
_____ Stepparent
_____ Neighbor
_____ Doctor
_____ Spiritual or religious leader

Sadness

I feel sad when I think about...

_____

_____

_____

_____

_____

_____

_____

_____

_____

_____

_____

Sometimes it is hard to talk about you and your death because…

_____

_____

_____

_____

_____

_____

_____

_____

_____

_____

When I miss you this helps…

_____

_____

_____

_____

_____

_____

_____

_____

_____

_____

_____

The hardest thing for me right now is…

_____

_____

_____

_____

_____

_____

_____

_____

_____

_____

_____

The thing that keeps me going now is...

_____

_____

_____

_____

_____

_____

_____

_____

_____

_____

On special occasions, I have noticed…

_____

_____

_____

_____

_____

_____

_____

_____

_____

_____

My Body

Some physical symptoms that I have noticed since you died are...

_____

_____

_____

_____

_____

_____

_____

_____

_____

I know that activities like exercise, music, sports, dancing, drawing, or writing help me feel better, so this is how I am taking care of myself since you died...

_____

_____

_____

_____

_____

_____

_____

_____

_____

_____

_____

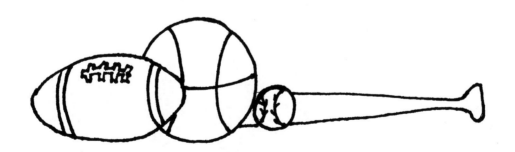

Guilt

Sometimes I think if these things had been different you might not have died...

_____

_____

_____

_____

_____

_____

_____

_____

_____

_____

_____

I know it is not my fault that you died, but sometimes I feel guilty about…

_____

_____

_____

_____

_____

_____

_____

_____

_____

_____

I wish I had not said or done these things…

_____

_____

_____

_____

_____

_____

_____

_____

_____

_____

I wish I had said or done these things…

_____

_____

_____

_____

_____

_____

_____

_____

_____

_____

This is what I think about why you died…

_____

_____

_____

_____

_____

_____

_____

_____

_____

_____

_____

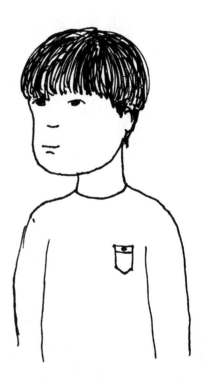

Anger

I sometimes feel angry when…

_____

_____

_____

_____

_____

_____

_____

_____

_____

_____

_____

Sometimes I feel angry about…

_____

_____

_____

_____

_____

_____

_____

_____

_____

_____

Some healthy ways I can express my anger are...

_____

_____

_____

_____

_____

_____

_____

_____

_____

_____

Fear

Sometimes I am afraid I will forget you because...

_____

_____

_____

_____

_____

_____

_____

_____

_____

_____

These are things I am afraid of now...

_____Loss

_____Being alone

_____Being criticized

_____Being out of control

_____Being abandoned

_____Success

_____Betrayal

_____Going crazy

_____Overwhelmed

_____Animals or insects

_____Failure

_____Being rejected

_____Being harmed or attacked

_____Illness or death

_____A specific person

Things I can do when I am feeling angry or sad...

_____Listen to music

_____Write music or a poem

_____Read

_____Write a letter

_____Draw or paint

_____Take pictures

_____Sew

_____Watch a movie

_____Pray or meditate

_____Clean

_____Play a computer or video game

_____Look at a photo album or pictures

_____Make a scrapbook

_____Work on a collection

_____Work on a puzzle

_____Work on a craft project or build something

_____Walk, hike, ride a bike, skate, or run

_____Exercise

_____Play with a pet

_____Sing a favorite song

_____Other

Acceptance And Hope

These are the things I look forward to...

_____

_____

_____

_____

_____

_____

_____

_____

_____

_____

These are some questions I would have liked to ask you and how I think you would have answered...

_____

_____

_____

_____

_____

_____

_____

_____

_____

_____

If I could talk to you, this is what I would say…

_____

_____

_____

_____

_____

_____

_____

_____

_____

_____

_____

This is how your life and death changed me and how I am different...

_____

_____

_____

_____

_____

_____

_____

_____

_____

_____

_____

"What we have once enjoyed, we can never lose. All that we love deeply becomes a part of us."

Helen Keller

These are some things that are different since you died...

_____

_____

_____

_____

_____

_____

_____

_____

_____

_____

The changes I least like are...

_____

_____

_____

_____

_____

_____

_____

_____

_____

_____

Here are my thoughts about what happens after a person dies...

_____

_____

_____

_____

_____

_____

_____

_____

_____

_____

The most important things I have learned since your death are...

_____

_____

_____

_____

_____

_____

_____

_____

_____

_____

"One who knows sorrow
For a long or little while
Learns a new language."

Jean Fox Holland

A ritual such as a candle lighting ceremony, planting a tree, creating a memorial park, painting a mural, attending a memorial service, a balloon launch, leaving gifts on the grave or the site of the death, or creating a plaque, poem, or song may be some things you will want to consider doing during this difficult time. Some people find that donating some money to a charity in memory of the person who died also helps.

This is how you will always be with me...

_____

_____

_____

_____

_____

_____

_____

_____

_____

_____

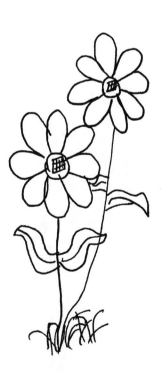

My thoughts and feelings about your death now...

_____

_____

_____

_____

_____

_____

_____

_____

_____

_____

_____

Some healthy ways I will respond to the next loss I experience are…

_____

_____

_____

_____

_____

_____

_____

_____

_____

_____

_____

Loss occurs frequently – learn from it.
Loss drains the spirit – seek solitude and sociality.
Loss can be put to work – help others.
Life is short – get on with your goals.
Life is NOW – enjoy the moment.

(Adapted from "Living With Loss," Faith at Work, April 1979.)

The Fence

The fence built of distrust,
    Was caused by hurt and pain.
She fenced others out,
    And then felt safe again.

She built the fence high,
    Then guarded the closed gate.
Afraid it would swing open,
    She sat there in wait.

Her head cried out "Not too close,"
    And fear was all about.
But she knew she had fenced herself in,
Trying to keep others out.

As time passed by,
    The emptiness crept in.
She wanted to open the gate,
    But where could she begin?

Trying to forget the hurt,
    Her heart begged, "Let them in."
But again her head cried out,
    "You will only be hurt again."

She knew the emptiness would go out,
    If she let people back in.
But throwing open the gate,
    Was not the way to begin.

She decided to open the gate,
A little at a time.
And sit and wait to see,
If everything was fine.

Some fear is still with her,
It has not completely gone away.
She knows she could be hurt again,
But will face it in a different way.

Andrea Sims

This is my good-bye letter to you…

Dear _____,

_____

_____

_____

_____

_____

_____

_____

_____

_____

_____

_____

_____

_____

_____

_____

_____

_____

_____

_____

_____

_____

_____

_____

_____

_____

_____

_____

_____

_____

_____

_____

_____

_____

_____

I will always remember you.

Love,

_____

Clues to knowing you are progressing in your journey through grief:

- ❑ You realize that some time has passed without your having thought about the loss
- ❑ You can concentrate on a book or on what others are saying again
- ❑ You make a new friend or reconnect with an old one
- ❑ You can remember both good and bad memories related to the loss
- ❑ You can focus on the present instead of dwelling on the past
- ❑ Your school grades improve
- ❑ You can return to normal activities and make some plans for the future
- ❑ You are eating and sleeping more like you were before the loss
- ❑ You don't feel so down on yourself
- ❑ You notice your surroundings more
- ❑ You feel like you can make decisions and solve problems again
- ❑ You have a sense of humor again and can laugh without feeling guilty
- ❑ You no longer feel tired all of the time
- ❑ You enjoy your friends again
- ❑ You can remember without it hurting so much
- ❑ You can help encourage others who are going through a loss

My Own Thoughts, Feelings, and Words

_____

_____

_____

_____

_____

_____

_____

_____

_____

_____

_____

_____

_____

_____

_____

_____

_____

_____

_____

_____

Books you may enjoy reading

- **A Taste Of Blackberries** by Doris Buchanan Smith
  A young boy suddenly loses his friend. This novel tells how he comes to grips with his grief. (Ages 5-10)
- **Annie And The Old One** by Miska Miles
  This is a beautifully illustrated story for children about change and death. Newberry Honor book. (Ages 7-9)
- **Blue Eyes Better** by Ruth Wallace-Brodeur
  Nothing seems real to 11 year old Tessa after her older brother is killed in a drunk driving accident. Tessa is forced to find a way to keep going. (Ages 10-14)
- **Bridge To Terabithia** by Katherine Paterson
  This Newberry Award Winner is the story of a friendship between a boy and girl and an ensuing tragedy. (Ages 8-12)
- **How It Feels When A Parent Dies** by Jill Krementz
  This is a collection of photo-essays with statements by eighteen bereaved children. (Ages 8-12)
- **Lifetimes** by Bryan Mellonie and Robert Ingpen
- **Tenth Good Thing About Barney** by Judith Viorst
  This illustrated book for children is about the death and burial of a pet cat. (Ages 5-10)
- **Two Of Them** by Aliki Brandenberg
  A girl and her grandfather share many happy times. She cares for him when he is sick, and remembers him when he dies.
- **Walk Two Moons** by Sharon Creech
  This winner of the Newberry Medal is a story of thirteen year old Sal, who traces the path of her missing mother from Ohio to Idaho with her grandparents. (Ages 10-14)
- **Why Did Grandpa Die?** By Barbara Shook Hazen
  This sensitive story shows children the comfort of sharing feelings, and

how the lasting links of memory can help to wash away the sadness of a death.